AMISH QUILTS

A BOOK OF POSTCARDS

AMISH QUILTS

Maker unknown
Broken Dishes (crib quilt), c. 1930
94 x 81.3 cm (37 x 32 in.)
Holmes County, Ohio
Collection of Faith and Stephen Brown

WWW.POMEGRANATE.COM

707 782 9000

Pomegranate

AMISH QUILTS

Rebecca Zook
Bars, c. 1910
210.8 x 193 cm (83 x 76 in.)
Lancaster County, Pennsylvania
Collection of Faith and Stephen Brown

707 782 9000   WWW.POMEGRANATE.COM

AMISH QUILTS

Maker unknown
Nine Patch, c. 1920
188 × 157.5 cm (74 × 62 in.)
Kalona, Iowa
Collection of Faith and Stephen Brown

707 782 9000   WWW.POMEGRANATE.COM

Pomegranate

AMISH QUILTS

Barbara Fisher
Center Diamond, c. 1900
208.3 × 208.3 cm (82 × 82 in.)
Lancaster County, Pennsylvania
Collection of Faith and Stephen Brown

707 782 9000   WWW.POMEGRANATE.COM

AMISH QUILTS

Maker unknown
Broken Star, c. 1930
203.2 x 193 cm (80 x 76 in.)
Holmes County, Ohio
Collection of Faith and Stephen Brown

707 782 9000   WWW.POMEGRANATE.COM

Pomegranate

AMISH QUILTS

Maker unknown
Crosses and Losses, 1898
203.2 × 175.3 cm (80 × 69 in.)
Holmes County, Ohio
Collection of Faith and Stephen Brown

707 782 9000   WWW.POMEGRANATE.COM

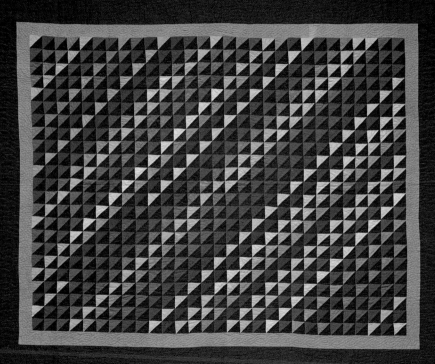

AMISH QUILTS

Maker unknown
Diagonal Triangles, c. 1930
203.2 x 172.7 cm (80 x 68 in.)
Holmes County, Ohio
Collection of Faith and Stephen Brown

707 782 9000   WWW.POMEGRANATE.COM

Pomegranate

AMISH QUILTS

Maker unknown
Tumbling Blocks, c. 1930
218.4 × 208.3 cm (86 × 82 in.)
Holmes County, Ohio
Collection of Faith and Stephen Brown

707 782 9000   WWW.POMEGRANATE.COM

Pomegranate

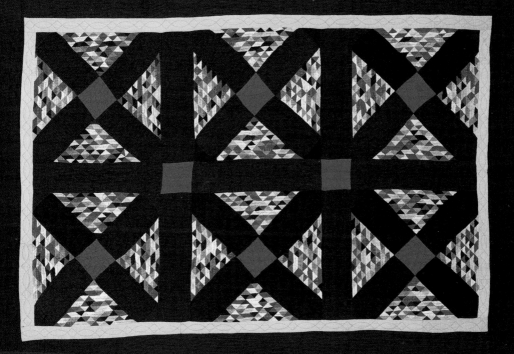

AMISH QUILTS

Maker unknown
Railroad Crossing, c. 1930
182.9 x 132.1 cm (72 x 52 in.)
Holmes County, Ohio
Collection of Faith and Stephen Brown

707 782 9000   WWW.POMEGRANATE.COM

Pomegranate

AMISH QUILTS

Maker unknown
Bowtie, c. 1930
215.9 × 190.5 cm (85 × 75 in.)
Holmes County, Ohio
Collection of Faith and Stephen Brown

707 782 9000   WWW.POMEGRANATE.COM

AMISH QUILTS

Maker unknown
Double Wedding Ring, c. 1920
198.1 × 165.1 cm (78 × 65 in.)
Holmes County, Ohio
Collection of Faith and Stephen Brown

707 782 9000   WWW.POMEGRANATE.COM

Pomegranate

AMISH QUILTS

Maker unknown
Ocean Waves, 1917
177.8 x 172.7 cm (70 x 68 in.)
Holmes County, Ohio
Collection of Faith and Stephen Brown

707 782 9000 WWW.POMEGRANATE.COM

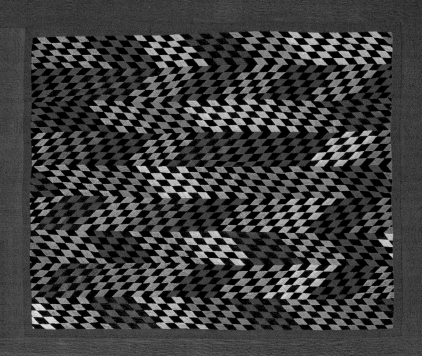

AMISH QUILTS

Maker unknown
Unnamed pattern, c. 1930
190.5 x 165.1 cm (75 x 65 in.)
Holmes County, Ohio
Collection of Faith and Stephen Brown

707 782 9000   WWW.POMEGRANATE.COM

AMISH QUILTS

Maker unknown
Old Maid's Puzzle, c. 1930
198.1 x 182.9 cm (78 x 72 in.)
Holmes County, Ohio
Collection of Faith and Stephen Brown

707 782 9000   WWW.POMEGRANATE.COM

AMISH QUILTS

Maker unknown
Nine Patch (crib quilt), c. 1940
127 x 106.7 cm (50 x 42 in.)
Midwest
Collection of Faith and Stephen Brown

707 782 9000   WWW.POMEGRANATE.COM

Pomegranate

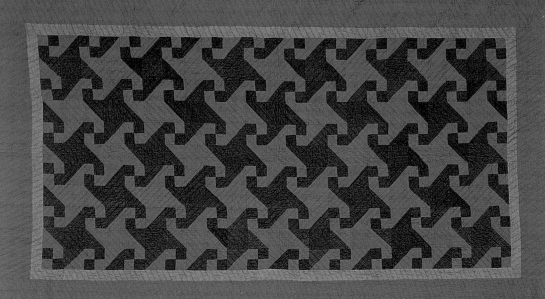

AMISH QUILTS

Maker unknown
Indiana Puzzle (youth quilt), c. 1930
200.7 x 116.8 cm (79 x 46 in.)
Midwest
Collection of Faith and Stephen Brown

707 782 9000 WWW.POMEGRANATE.COM

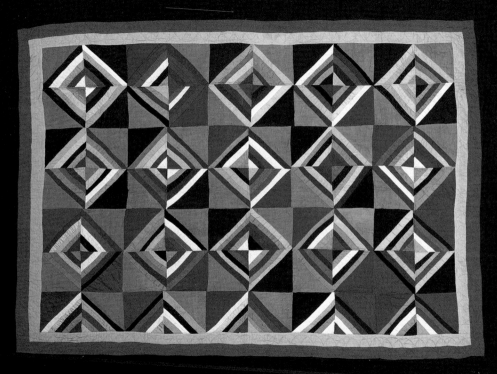

AMISH QUILTS

Maker unknown
Roman Stripe, c. 1930
218.4 x 165.1 cm (86 x 65 in.)
Holmes County, Ohio
Collection of Faith and Stephen Brown

707 782 9000   WWW.POMEGRANATE.COM

AMISH QUILTS

Maker unknown
Ocean Waves, c. 1925
226.1 x 193 cm (89 x 76 in.)
Holmes County, Ohio
Collection of Faith and Stephen Brown

707 782 9000   WWW.POMEGRANATE.COM

Pomegranate

AMISH QUILTS

Maker unknown
Pine Trees (crib quilt), c. 1930
142.2 x 94 cm (56 x 37 in.)
Holmes County, Ohio
Collection of Faith and Stephen Brown

707 782 9000   WWW.POMEGRANATE.COM

Pomegranate

AMISH QUILTS

Maker unknown
Sunshine and Shadow, c. 1930
226.1 x 218.4 cm (89 x 86 in.)
Lancaster County, Pennsylvania
Collection of Faith and Stephen Brown

707 782 9000   WWW.POMEGRANATE.COM

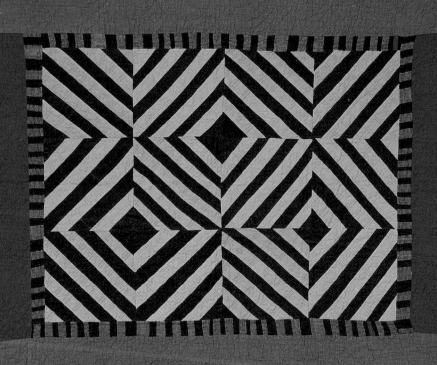

AMISH QUILTS

Maker unknown
Roman Stripe variation (crib quilt), c. 1915
114.3 × 94 cm (45 × 37 in.)
Kansas
Collection of Faith and Stephen Brown

707 782 9000   WWW.POMEGRANATE.COM

Pomegranate

AMISH QUILTS

Maker unknown
Unnamed pattern (crib quilt), c. 1930
76.2 × 63.5 cm (30 × 25 in.)
Somerset County, Pennsylvania
Collection of Faith and Stephen Brown

WWW.POMEGRANATE.COM

707 782 9000

Pomegranate

AMISH QUILTS

Maker unknown
Unnamed pattern (crib quilt), c. 1930
99.1 x 88.9 cm (39 x 35 in.)
Holmes County, Ohio
Collection of Faith and Stephen Brown

707 782 9000   WWW.POMEGRANATE.COM

Pomegranate

AMISH QUILTS

Maker unknown
Log Cabin, Barn Raising variation (crib quilt), c. 1925
88.9 × 66 cm (35 × 26 in.)
Arthur, Illinois
Collection of Faith and Stephen Brown

707 782 9000   WWW.POMEGRANATE.COM

Pomegranate

AMISH QUILTS

Maker unknown
Triangles (crib quilt), c. 1930
104.1 x 83.8 cm (41 x 33 in.)
Kalona, Iowa
Collection of Faith and Stephen Brown

707 782 9000   WWW.POMEGRANATE.COM

Pomegranate

AMISH QUILTS

Maker unknown
Lattice (crib quilt), c. 1930
134.6 x 109.2 cm (53 x 43 in.)
Haven, Kansas
Collection of Faith and Stephen Brown

707 782 9000 WWW.POMEGRANATE.COM

Pomegranate

AMISH QUILTS

Maker unknown
Center Diamond, c. 1930
203.2 × 203.2 cm (80 × 80 in.)
Lancaster County, Pennsylvania
Collection of Faith and Stephen Brown

707 782 9000   WWW.POMEGRANATE.COM

Pomegranate

AMISH QUILTS

Ada Gingerich
Bricks in Bars, c. 1930
193 x 116.8 cm (76 x 46 in.)
Arthur, Illinois
Collection of Faith and Stephen Brown

707 782 9000   WWW.POMEGRANATE.COM

Pomegranate

AMISH QUILTS

Maker unknown
Thirty-Six Patch variation (crib quilt), c. 1930
83.8 x 78.7 cm (33 x 31 in.)
Arthur, Illinois
Collection of Faith and Stephen Brown

707 782 9000 WWW.POMEGRANATE.COM

Pomegranate

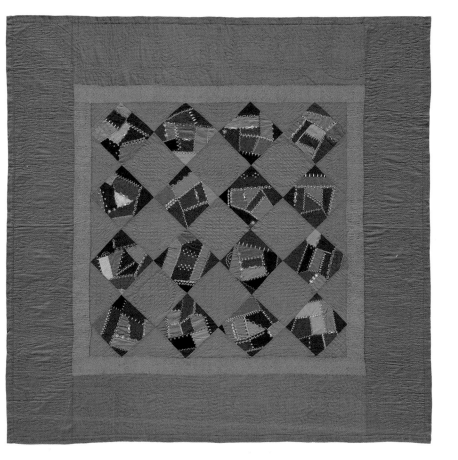

AMISH QUILTS

Maker unknown
Crazy Quilt, c. 1930
208.3 x 203.2 cm (82 x 80 in.)
Lancaster, Pennsylvania
Collection of Faith and Stephen Brown

707 782 9000   WWW.POMEGRANATE.COM

Pomegranate

AMISH
QUILTS

A BOOK OF POSTCARDS

Pomegranate
SAN FRANCISCO

Pomegranate Communications, Inc.
Box 808022, Petaluma CA 94975
800 227 1428; www.pomegranate.com

Pomegranate Europe Ltd.
Unit 1, Heathcote Business Centre, Hurlbutt Road
Warwick, Warwickshire CV34 6TD, UK
[+44] 0 1926 430111; sales@pomeurope.co.uk

ISBN 978-0-7649-5172-5
Pomegranate Catalog No. AA614

Pomegranate publishes books of postcards on a wide range of subjects.
Please contact the publisher for more information.

Cover designed by Gina Bostian
Printed in Korea
18 17 16 15 14 13 12 11 10 09   10 9 8 7 6 5 4 3 2 1

To facilitate detachment of the postcards from this book, fold each card along its perforation line before tearing.